THEIR Must

Bee Sum

Weigh TOO

No *Witch* Is

the Rite Whey

THEIR Must *Bee* Sum Weigh TOO No *Witch* Is the Rite Whey

Challenging Exercises to Evaluate Your Grammar and Writing Skills

Linda Robinson Hinnant

AnnotationPress
A Division of WinePress Publishing

Annotation Press (a division of WinePress Publishing, PO Box 428, Enumclaw, WA 98022) functions only as book publisher. As such, the ultimate design, content, editorial accuracy, and views expressed or implied in this work are those of the author.

The author of this book has waived the publisher's suggested editing services. As such, the author is responsible for any errors found in this finished product.

ISBN 13: 978-1-59977-030-7
ISBN 10: 1-59977-030-X
Library of Congress Catalog Card Number: 2011929600

Dear Kevin,
Keep doing all
you do !!

This book is dedicated to my special firsts:
God, Mom, Dad (JT),
my husband Kenneth and Toni

BEING CONCISE AND explicit in writing helps the reader in understanding your thoughts. Word choice is important in giving visual and sensory impact to them. For example, if you overuse the adjective "good," how does one sense differences between a good **dog,** a good **meal**, a good **book**, or a good **parent**? An **obedient** dog, a **delicious** meal, a **suspenseful** book, and an **understanding** parent are connotative and engaging. Aside from the universality of our daily computer use and its growing jargon, other changes have been made in communication techniques, compelling many to use what is termed "politically correct" language. Many of us learned formal English before these were issues to be addressed. We still know that "him" and "he" refer to a single human being—male or female. If it is

THEIR MUST BEE SUM WEIGH TOO NO
WITCH IS THE RITE WHEY

your preference to be "politically correct" **(PC)** in your writing, do so. But, notwithstanding these frequent changes in language and communication methods, find all errors of grammar, spelling, word choice/terminology, ambiguity, punctuation, capitalization, redundancy, logic, and syntax in the following sentences using formal English and write the correction(s). If no errors, answer "none". Rewrite a sentence(s) only if necessary to correct its structure, eliminate ambiguity, or other mandatory clarification. The corrections/answers are at the end of the book in **BOLD** print. Remember, the **objective** is not if you could have written the sentence better or would have differently, but **DO YOU FIND ERRORS IN THESE??!!! DON'T PEEK AT ANSWERS UNTIL YOU HAVE FINISHED OR YOU WILL CHEAT YOURSELF.**

1. You believing in yourself is the first step necessary to being successful.
2. My Uncle Patrick who's silly nickname is P man caught thirty trout last weekend.
3. We learned in elementary school that the earth was round.
4. Although the coroner found drugs in her organs, her late husband said she had never used drugs.
5. My husband and best friend is being honored at the ball.
6. Many of the people speaking were friends of Mia's.

7. How many cites were sited in the report of alien sightings.

8. The two twins didn't like being dressed identical for school.

9. Don't take the Lord's name in vane.

10. What you did it is unholy for a man of God.

11. Tell everyone here accept the ushers to leave early.

12. I won't bet one scent that this cite will be better for there wedding.

13. There have been many accidents caused by deers running into traffic.

14. Twenty is printed on Domonique's uniform shirt.

15. The Williams sisters' plan to become minority owners of the Miami Dolphins.

16. The coroner ruled that a fatal combination of drugs given to Michael killed him.

17. All the peoples of the world must respect the earth for us to survive.

18. The airplanes were placed in hangers to prevent accumulation of ice on them.

19. We'll be talking to his former ex-mother in law.

20. I was originally born in Ohio, but now live in Detroit.

21. Who's turn is it to get desert for our meal today?

22. My neighbor, who won the lottery, donated to the church she plans to join.

23. Prior to becoming president, Michelle Obama made more money than Barack.

24. Joe was responsible for the death of five people.

25. She felt alright after he apologized to her.

26. Each of the thousand protesters is hoping for better wages and hours.

27. After talking about yesterday's weather, the weatherman said, Let's move forward and talk about the weather outside today.

28. The man found a hidden painting of da Vinci's underneath another painting.

29. Not everyone likes champagne dessert dry.

30. I pray daily for President Obama to have at least one opportunity daily to pray in uninterrupted solitude.

31. I sincerely want to give my three children a better life than I had.

32. Whichever team score the most points will play the bonus round.

33. The doctor who performed her emergency surgery was Dr. Wilson.

34. John used to rale against his parents with hypocricy until his brother's violent death provided him an epifany.

35. His mother wants to see that every returning soldier get what he needs to readjust.

36. My son learned the alphabets before he was one year's old.

37. My daughter who loves traveling more than her sister opened a travel agency.

38. Any organizations or candidate wanting the Black vote must prove their belief in democracy.

39. The number of death in Japan has now raised to over 25,000.

40. My children hanged Christmas wreaths on all the windows.

41. Guatemala, Honduras, and El Salvador the Northern Triangle are exploiting borders to transport illegal drugs.

42. Each jurors collective passions, objectivity, and wisdom is needed for a fair verdict.

43. My family and I were already to leave when Kyla got sick.

44. Because of Emmy's exotic beauty she was attracted to most men.

45. It seems that people want to politicize even aspects of religion.

46. Hundreds of F.B.I. and police are looking for the sniper as we speak.

47. Today our English teacher Mrs. Delores Ester told us to take our literature journals to class tomorrow.

48. I lost more than was necessary had I came when they started the actor selections.

49. I don't want to give the government nothing I don't have to.

50. It was announced that John Smitheon and Joseph Bangle might resign in order to spend more time with his family.

51. That lady through acid on her own face. Why would someone do that to themselves?

52. The parents of the girl killed by the driver texting couldn't get a law passed to make it illegal to text while driving, but they got the speed limit changed through the street where she was killed.

53. Zuzzi is one of the few women in the choir who sing a cappella.

54. When my symptoms got worst I went back to my doctor again.

55. Have you forgotten that god was in your life daily?

56. My award winning aunt along with her twins is the hostess of the affair.

57. There were less people at the press conference than we expected.

58. The United States allows many foreigners to emigrate each year.

59. We planted annuals in the front yard to avoid planting flowers each year.

60. I got my bachelor's and undergraduate degrees at Howard University.

61. The mystery about the errors at Arlington Cemetery grave sights continue.

62. Do you conversate with your boyfriend everyday?

63. Many drugstores give free flu shots, making it easier for everyone to get theirs.

64. This initiative established the District of Columbia as one of only two states with a totally community

based system for persons with developmental disabilities.

65. No one is sinless, but we all should strive to sinless.

66. Who do you like best, Fred or his brother?

67. The human body is an amazing machine consists of two hundred and six bones, with over fifty of them in the hands.

68. Christians read the bible to learn and understand God's percepts to avoid sin.

69. Grandpa told us about the many innocent Negroes hung for lies told on them.

70. Do you play tennis better than her?

71. We pay fewer tax under Obama than Bush.

72. To be safe always hope for the best, but plan for the worse.

73. Maintenance crews use seperate devices to clean the dome of the Capital.

74. I shouldn't have hanged that leather coat on the thin rack.

75. My husband selected Carmen Ambrosio, not me, to be our children's nanny.

76. The levee might not hole because it has rained for the last eight days.

77. Knowledge of the high numbers of court martial of Negro soldiers was guarded.

78. For a mom or dad who are trying to spend more time with their children, we need to provide better paying jobs with decent hours.

79. Thankfully, not one of the passengers were hurt in the plane crash.

80. We counted just three cows, two roosters, four oxes, and twenty one chickens on the farm.

81. Unfortunately, there is war or other fighting in too many countries around the world.

82. I like to play different games, but chess is more harder for me to learn.

83. You're wrong. That is her son being honored as a hero!

84. This is your decision to make, no matter what any of them say.

85. The current incumbent governor must decide on costly transportation needs.

86. President Obama has faced crucial phenomenon his entire time in office.

87. My adult son still put small paper trash in my purse rather then litter.

88. Mr. Floyd is preceded in death by his wife.

89. The star player reflected back on who helped him achieve his skills and success.

90. How many women said she make a fool of herself over a man?

91. The committee decided a discussion between he and his opponent might help eliminate some of the hostility shown in the pass.

92. Truly, I do not know if ghosts are real

93. Gibbs helped Gabriel Harper a friend of his deceased daughter's to prove that he wasn't guilty.

94. I didn't waive away my rights to that property when we got divorced.

95. Cookies and milk is the snack I leave for Santa each year.

96. In my library books are arranged as fiction, religion, history, and travel.

97. Reverend John Thomas, my loving father, counseled my husband and I about love and marriage using the bible, his constant companion.

98. Mary's mom told her that her nails were too long and she cut them down.

99. Ms. Lottie Hughes, my old High School English teacher, taught me to like Shakespeare works more than my new teacher does.

100. I wanted to go back to school after I became a mother again.

101. In Arlington where I grew up that was the suburbs.

102. My children frequently loose their gloves and hats.

103. Many people ask me, "Are those your fingernails?"

104. For fourty years I been researching my family's genealogy.

105. Are you sure none of them know about the surprise?

106. My hands are rough because I frequently use pads with a high level of alcohol that is very dry.

107. It was him and his brother who tried to change my mind about the reward money.

108. My brother was teased because he didn't have a girl friend to take to the prom.

109. The view is dark now, but it's lightning fast as the sun comes up.

110. I can't hardly hear you because the music is too loud.

111. Sixty Minutes is my dad's favorite television program.

112. Many students inferred that I was mean because I commanded discipline.

113. The book Mrs. Pauline Harper assigned was real hard for me to understand.

114. A coalition of more than 350 groups expect to march for jobs.

115. Mabel's sweet daughter has to medically fight all her two little years of life.

116. A preverse man sows discord freely.

117. Because my aunt Kim is more pregnant than my wife, we listen to her advice.

118. Even if you've never sang in a choir before, please join one of ours.

119. I know that five plus seven are twelve.

120. Carl Farmer Jr. went looking for Derrick Butler his friend and his coworker.

121. You need to read Peggy Nicholson's new book, "Jim Crow Is A Buzzard."

122. One of my daughter's teacher's, Anna Robinson, is an Olympic finalist.

123. The burglars broke into school and took several stolen items needed for my class.

124. Why did he refuse the lessened penalty that the judge Connie Morgan offered?

125. A single coin found led to the 2011 discovery of a ship that sunk in 1539 with many valuables found intact.

126. Victims of car accidents try to quickly get to a hospital that can save their life.

127. She pulled off the mask I had wore to disguise myself.

128. The choir practice every Tuesday and Thursday.

129. Who's cell phone was ringing during the funeral service?

130. I'm not sure where the temperature is right now.

131. A friend of my mother's past away yesterday from cancer.

132. The wife of an Egyptian born U.S. citizen learned he's a suspected terrorist.

133. All mother-in-laws should be treated with love and respect.

134. Celebrate the differences that makes each of us unique.

135. The guards propenisity for errors cost him life.

136. I should read more, go shopping for bargains, and conserve energy daily.

137. The volunteers bought all the donated goods to the church yesterday.

138. The two editor in chiefs honored the reporter for his subjective writing, which was impartial although it dealt with his father's business.

139. Being dedicated to our race as Frederick Douglass was is what I inspire to do.

140. The founder and CEO of the organization along with hundreds of supporters have made many improvements in the areas of need.

141. DelRico and Onari live further down the street than me.

142. The pastor Blossie Staten used an illusion of Moses in her sermon.

143. Did anybody beside you collect any clothing for the charity affair?

144. That data about the ten Chineses living in the hotel was unvaluable to the attorney.

145. Alicia gained so much weight that her dress busted at the seams.

146. Are all charter schools meeting the academic needs of citizens' students like Eagle Academy is?

147. She knows three languages, but speaks only spanish fluent.

148. Because of their expence, I had to reuse the same catheters for the rest of my life.

149. When president Obama took office I thanked God I lived to witness it.

150. My mom got one of them new digital cameras as a gift.

151. Just try and relax before you give the speech to the class.

152. I read where the new stadium will cause us not to get a library addition.

153. The unemployed technicians morals dropped because of their dim financial status.

154. She is Cassandra Pinkney, my dearest friend whom I met in the fourth grade.

155. None of the fighters did very good at the practice match.

156. At first, we couldn't see nothing in the blinding snow.

157. Beatrice Carter she is my dance partner.

158. Bishop Richard Allen, born a slave, was allowed to buy his freedom and later with preacher Absolom Jones, other ex-slaves, and Quakers, formed the Free Africa Society.

159. True love always pays attention and is shaped by those who love you and who you love.

160. Why do you think they're are signing up for kick boxing class.

161. Read I Corinthians 13, verses 4 through 7 to know what God says love is.

162. That license on the counter is my son's, Collin's.

163. The article stated that thousands implied for it yet only one will get the job.

164. I learned that styrofoam and plastic straws will never decompose.

165. If I was going to any foreign country I would study about it first.
166. The doctor urged fifty five year old men to get a prostrate examination.
167. There was a preceived assumption of the wife's affair by her husband.
168. The hospital will give an update on the condition of the twenty shooting victims.
169. You need to stop being so disrespected of your elders.
170. Organizing underwear by different items in a chester drawers is helpful.
171. Two many children have cavities in their tooth from eating to much candy and not brushing.
172. How many state of emergencies were called because of the severe storm?
173. How did she react to them scamming her grand mother out of her house?
174. If one of my children was gay I'd still love him.
175. Ted Williams needs more time to adjust to his sudden notoriety, reacquaint with his family, and decrease the media exposure.
176. "Delores is next door visiting with my mom, but I came here to let you know that I loved her so you'd approve of us still dating."
177. The governor said he asked the parole board to review Paul Brown's request for early release and that they supported it.

178. I shouldn't have ran so fast but as chairmen I had to equipt each participant with conservation techniques we use.

179. Linda's and Toni's mother taught the sisters as teenagers about credit card use.

180. It is the whole town who is grieving over the senseless shootings.

181. Meredith asked Rechar if he was a close friend of Diamond Staten's.

182. The most interesting animals to me are tigers, lions, kangaroos, snakes, gorillas, bears, antelope, cheetahs, camels, and elephants.

183. My brother hit hisself in the eye and told my farther I hit him.

184. There were many thiefs looting the homes of people that evacuated.

185. Fred Hopkins said, Linda Hinnant just shouted I was hugged by President Obama!

186. A gambler, a disbarred attorney, a lady with a penchant for setting fires, a runaway teen, a man strung out on alcohol, and a minister are members of my faith counseling group.

187. The two babys mothers were in the waiting room while tests were preformed.

188. You use too many ands in your writings.

189. Independence Day, July 4, is not the day slaves received freedom. They named June 19th as Juneteenth, the day freedom was granted to them

by the Emancipation Proclamation, although it took two and a half years before they all were freed.

190. This is a too heavily loaded wagon for the display.

191. I wake up every morning at four o clock daily by habit not an alarm clock.

192. He served us a dinner wearing a butlers' suit.

193. Do you know who discovered the traffic light?

194. The candidates speak like they've all ready been elected.

195. Janice screamed and her husband fainted respectfully when their son was born.

196. Can I drive your car to the store?

197. It took a long time for her husband to get over the betrayal. I'm still not sure he hasn't.

198. God doesn't cause everything that happens, but he allows all that happens.

199. We slept past the clock's ringing and missed our flight.

200. Sitting in the passenger seat the monuments were clearly seen.

201. A wood burning stove it needs wood added often to thrive.

202. A married couple should be amendable to counseling before ending their marriage.

203. The six lifes lost in the Arizona shooting caused much pain to many.

204. Susan learns of Mary's affair while celebrating her job promotion.

205. A group of college students discover a dark secret while visiting Spain.

206. Did your condo or home need repairs after the earthquake?

207. The lethal injection didn't kill him completely in the designated time, making it illegal to now try it again.

208. Another person has died after being struck and killed by a hit and run driver.

209. The fact that I've been driving for five years to your twenty-one, doesn't factor into me giving better directions than you do.

210. Though he was found to be innocent twenty years later, John Peters was convicted of murder because witnesses prevaricated and Peters court appointed lawyer wasn't aggressive in his presentation.

211. Only one of the hundred listeners has won a prize today.

212. The sly but clever paparazzi waited in the lake to get his picture of the star.

213. The young woman refused to cooperate during Det. Brittany Thorne's investigation of her brutal rape.

214. I really don't think man knows how many types of fishes exist.

215. Anita Ford, not Carla Berry and her friend are going to the show with me.

216. If everyone asks for a seating change on this flight it will be impossible to please him.

217. His cousins have stole things since they were teenagers.

218. Mr. Randolph Ivey drove passed the cemetery he alone cared for it's five decades of existence with pride.

219. Would you sit the dishes on the counter for me?

220. Which history coarse did you take in seventh grade?

221. My sister does well in grammer, but I like math better.

222. My two-year-old toddler falls often.

223. I raked all the leafs in the front and back yard today.

224. The girls alumni meeting is held every Wedensday.

225. The advanced science class does homework at different levels.

226. The longer slavery exists increasing many states economy owners became less eglatarian.

227. I think neither of the parents realize the severity of John's expulsion.

228. Laws are needed to punish crimes committed on the internet.

229. She's not going to look like she does when she's fifty years old.

230. She still babies her children though they are all adults now.

231. The teens viewed the jobs offered to them at the job fair as worthless then those offered to young adults.

232. This summer I walked more miles than at any time in my life.

233. The end of the world as envisioned by Christianity, Judaism, and Islam are being studied by the scholars.

234. Statistics show one in five teenagers consider suicide.

235. Although John's a friend of the President's, I wanted to meet his wife the President's cousin, who has more clout with him.

236. His brother has cancer and died a week before the wedding.

237. Japan's 2011 earthquake and tsunami is generating a high death rate.

238. Dad learned in 1862 Congress enacts the nation's first income tax law.

239. The church's mourning service is shorter than the evening service.

240. How is the public handling the man's threat to bomb a bus on Facebook?

241. I pay complements to people I feel deserves them.

242. The Negro League ball players were.

243. The tiles with pictures and names were so expertly layed you couldn't see where one ended and another began.

244. We found an antique, wooden chest at the yard sell.

245. I don't have no water in my thermos.

246. The investigators think there is more to the story than he's admitting to.

247. Did you ever buy yourself some stationary with engraved initials?

248. Many selfishless people give to those who are in need.

249. The government definitely needs to trim its budget back.

250. There must be some thing I can do to assist the family.

251. A tractor crashed thru a ramp and trapped the driver inside and it then dangled precarious over a crowded highway beneath it for two hours.

252. We bought the sofa at Hecht's with a matching foot stool.

253. My sister Toni set an exemplary model I still try to imulate though she's been in heaven seventeen years.

254. A group of friends try to plan their twenty fifth high school reunion in Hawaii.

255. We need to be congizant that our grandparents might not know what it means if we tell them to google or tweet some thing.

256. Amalgamated bank, who underwrote our church construction, is very generous.

257. Three quarters of his house were destroyed by the fierce winds.

258. I loaned Kenny's and mines boat to Drayton last weekend.
259. This forecast is what the weather for the weekend will be today.
260. Can you sign as well as him to the deaf?
261. Please lay completely still during the test.
262. This room smells badly.
263. I should have laid down when I got home to rest my body.
264. Is your brother the fearfullest in the group?
265. I exited out the closest of the rooms two doors.
266. We were formally known as the Bees, but now as the Butterflys.
267. The speeding driver breaked when the police started following him.
268. A tsunami is like a high sea wave following an earthquake.
269. I graduated from Brown junior high school in 1964.
270. Frequent errors found in measuring people's radiation exposure at airports may change the way people fly.
271. Upon entering federal buildings your medals are placed in a screening basket.
272. Those kind of tires are usually on sports cars.
273. After reading the paragraph over again it still wasn't logical to me.

274. How old do you have to be in Texas to not be considered a miner?

275. Kenneth Rooks lead Emmy to classes the first day because she was unfamiliar with the new school.

276. The small but densely peopled Nigeria village we visited lacked drinking water, food, and medicine for its few inhabitants.

277. I did have some mispelled words on the pamplet

278. Being an adolecent isn't ecstacy for anyone.

279. "My fellow Americans, said President Obama opening his speech let me assure you that our economic situation will change for the better in time.

280. My sister loves shrimps, french fries, and doughnuts.

281. I know how to sign, but not as well as him.

282. Me and Imelda went to the islands without our husbands.

283. But when we like him realizes the importance of our history a dissimiliar Renaissance for us will begin.

284. While reading the book a man named White I was enlightened.

285. The woman fixed theirselves ribs, greens, and macaroni, and cheese.

286. A teenage girl told me that my diamond ring is bling.

287. I'd give you the world if it was mine to give.

288. We want all students to be apart of the earth friendly initiative.

289. Breathing is one of the few things man does continually.
290. Passengers arriving from Japan are giving a screen test to detect radiation.
291. As I drove around the mountains the steep clifts came into view.
292. Neither of the cars are in the garage.
293. The biggest problem with roses are wilting.
294. The class is going home because of the water leaking in the room.
295. Either the principle or the teachers is responsible for this error.
296. Recognizing the differences between twins are difficult for many.
297. Dr. Carter G. Woodson found the Association for the Study of African American Life and History (ASALH) in 1915.
298. Outside of the white house it was warmer than inside.
299. The real housewives of DC have been cancelled after one season.
300. We must fight for our unalienable rights or loose them.

THEIR MUST BEE SUM WEIGH TOO NO
WITCH IS THE RITE WHEY

BONUS:

Hopefully, you successfully mastered the sentences and were pleased with the objective of this book. Therefore, you will have no difficulty finding five complete sentences in the following words by placing a period at the end of each; **nothing else is permitted.**

I never saw his one-eyed tigers are his logo trademark is a legal identification a manufacturer uses any tactic to sell his clothing a necessity of life is air

ANSWERS FOR SENTENCES

THE **BOLD** WORDS or a new sentence is provided as the correction(s) needed.

1. **Your** believing
2. Patrick**,**   **whose** man**,**
3. earth **is**
4. **omit late**
5. **none**
6. **Mia**
7. **sites** were **cited** sightings?
8. **omit two**   **identically**
9. **vain**
10. **omit it**
11. **except**
12. one **cent** this **site** **their**

13. deer
14. "Twenty"
15. sisters
16. omit fatal
17. none
18. hangars
19. omit ex-   mother-in-law
20. omit originally
21. Whose   dessert
22. omit commas
23. Rewrite– **Michelle Obama made more money than Barack prior to his becoming President.** OR **Barack Obama made less money than Michelle Obama before he became President.**
24. **is** responsible   **deaths**
25. all right
26. none
27. "Let's   omit outside   today."
28. of **da Vinci**
29. **desert** dry
30. none
31. I **have** had
32. scores
33. **is** Dr.
34. rail   hypocrisy   epiphany
35. gets   he or she needs
36. alphabet   year

37. It depends on writer's meaning— **My daughter who loves traveling more than her sister does opened a travel agency.** OR **My daughter who loves traveling more than she loves her sister opened a travel agency.**
38. **(PC) his or her** belief
39. **deaths** has now **risen**
40. **hung**
41. Salvador, Triangle ,
42. **juror's** **are** needed
43. **all ready**
44. **attractive**
45. **none**
46. **FBI agents**
47. teacher, Ester, **bring** our
48. I **come**
49. government **anything** have to **give**
50. **their families**
51. **threw** acid would **she** to **herself**
52. **on** the street
53. **sings**
54. **worse** omit back to OR **again**
55. **God is**
56. **award-winning** aunt, twins,
57. **fewer** people
58. **immigrate**
59. **perennials**
60. use **bachelor** OR **undergraduate** degree

61. **sites   continues**
62. **converse   every day**
63. get **one**
64. **Change states** to **governments** (DC is not a state)
    community-based
65. strive to **sin less**
66. **Whom   better**
67. **consisting**
68. **Bible   precepts**
69. **hanged**
70. than **she**
71. **less** tax   than **under** Bush
72. **worst**
73. **separate   Capitol**
74. **hung**
75. **My husband, not I, selected Carmen Ambrosio
    to be our children's nanny**.
76. **hold**
77. **number   court-martials**
78. who **is**   with **her or his** children
79. **was** hurt
80. **oxen   twenty-one**
81. **omit around the world**
82. **omit more**
83. **none**
84. **says**
85. use either **current** or **incumbent**
86. **phenomena**

87. **puts** rather **than**
88. **none**
89. **omit back**
90. **How many women said they make/made fools of themselves over a man?**
91. between **him** in the **past**
92. **omit are real exist.**
93. **Harper, daughter, isn't** guilty
94. **omit away**
95. **none**
96. **library,**
97. and **me Bible**
98. **specify** who **she** is— **Mary cut** OR **her mom cut** omit **down**
99. **former high school inspired** me **Shakespeare's** or **Shakespearean current** teacher does
100. after I **had another child**
101. **omit that**
102. **lose** their
103. your **natural fingernails** or **are those artificial fingernails** (Either belongs to the person)
104. **forty** I **have** been **omit family's**
105. **knows**
106. very **drying**
107. was **he**
108. **girlfriend**
109. **lightening**
110. **can** hardly

111. **Sixty Minutes**
112. **implied** that
113. **omit real hard**   was **difficult** for me
114. **expects**
115. **Mabel's sweet daughter has had to fight medically her two short years of life.**
116. **perverse**
117. **Because my Aunt Kim is further into her pregnancy than my wife is, we listen to her advice.**
118. **sung**
119. **is** twelve
120. **Farmer, Jr.   Butler,   omit the second his**
121. *Jim Crow Is A Buzzard*
122. If only one daughter use **daughter's teachers** OR if two or more daughters use **daughters' teachers**
123. **omit stolen**
124. **lesser**   omit second **the**   **Judge**
125. **sank**
126. try to **get quickly**   **lives**
127. had **worn**
128. **practices**
129. **whose** cell
130. **what** the temperature
131. **mother**   **passed**
132. **Egyptian-born**
133. **mothers-in-law**
134. **make**
135. **guard's**   **propensity**   him **his**

136. **shop** for
137. **brought**
138. **editors in chief**   **objective** writing
139. **aspire** to do
140. **has** made
141. **farther**   than **I**
142. **allusion to**
143. **besides**
144. **Chinese**   **invaluable**
145. **burst**
146. citizens' **children**
147. **Spanish**   **fluently**
148. **expense**   **I'll have** to reuse
149. **President**
150. got one of **those**
151. try **to** relax
152. read **that**
153. **technicians'**   **morales**
154. **Pinkney, friend,**
155. very **well**
156. **could** see
157. **omit she**
158. **none**
159. and **whom** you
160. **omit are**   class?
161. **13:4–7**
162. **none**
163. **applied** for it,

164. **Styrofoam**
165. **were** going
166. **fifty-five-year-old** prostate
167. **perceived**
168. **conditions**
169. **disrespectful**
170. **chest of** drawers
171. **Too** teeth **too** much candy
172. **states** emergency
173. **their** scamming **grandmother**
174. **is** gay love **him or her**
175. **to** reacquaint **to** decrease
176. **love** her of **our** still
177. **omit that they** support it
178. have **run** fast, **chairman (PC) chairperson** to **equip**
179. **Linda and Toni's**
180. town **that** is
181. **is** a friend **Staten**
182. **are:**
183. **himself** father
184. **thieves** who evacuated
185. **"Linda** shouted, 'I was Obama!' "
186. **A gambler, a disbarred attorney, a female pyro-maniac, a runaway teenager, an alcoholic and a minister are members of my faith-counseling group.**
187. **babies'** performed

188. **"and's"**
189. **none**
190. **too-heavily**
191. **omit daily** OR **every morning   o'clock   habit,**
    not **by** an
192. **Wearing a butler's suit, he served us dinner.**
193. who **invented** the
194. **already**
195. **respectively**
196. **May** I
197. he **has**
198. **He** allows
199. **slept past**
200. **Sitting in the passenger seat, I clearly saw the monuments.**
201. **wood-burning   omit it**
202. **amenable**
203. **lives**
204. **While celebrating her job promotion, Susan learns of Mary's affair.** (Susan has the promotion and Mary has the affair in this sentence; you would exchange the names' order in the sentence to reverse this first meaning.)
205. **discovers**
206. or **house**
207. **omit completely** and **now   prescribed** time
208. **omit and killed**
209. **omit** comma   **my** giving

210. Peters's   court-appointed
211. none
212. paparazzo
213. of **the woman's** rape
214. none
215. friend,   **is** going
216. **If all the passengers on this flight request a seating change it will be impossible to oblige them all.**
217. stolen
218. drove **past**   alone **has cared**   its
219. set
220. course
221. grammar
222. none
223. leaves   yards
224. girls'   Wednesday
225. do
226. existed,   states'   economies,   egalitarian
227. realizes
228. **Laws are needed to punish people committing crimes on the Internet.**
229. she does **now**
230. omit now
231. worth less   than
232. any **other** time
233. **is** being studied
234. considers

235. **Although John's a friend of the President, I wanted to meet John's wife, the President's cousin, who has more clout with the President.**

236. **had** cancer

237. **are** generating   death **toll**

238. **that** in 1862   **enacted**

239. **morning**

240. threat **on Facebook** to bomb a bus

241. **compliments   deserve**

242. **This is a sentence fragment; complete the thought.**

243. **laid   ends   begins**

244. **omit comma**   yard **sale**

245. **any** water   OR omit **no**

246. **omit to** after admitting

247. **stationery**

248. **selfless** OR **unselfish** people

249. **omit back**

250. **something** (as one word)

251. **After a tractor crashed through a ramp, trapping the driver inside, it dangled precariously over a crowded highway for two hours.**

252. sofa **with a matching foot stool at**

253. **emulate   Heaven**

254. **While in Hawaii, a group of friends tries to plan their twenty-fifth high school reunion.** OR **A group of friends tries to plan for their twenty-fifth high school reunion to be held in Hawaii.**

255. **cognizant   Google   something**
256. **Bank   which** underwrote **church's**
257. **was** destroyed
258. Kenny's and **my**
259. **This is today's forecast for the weekend weather.**
260. **he**
261. **lie**
262. **bad**
263. have **lain**
264. **most fearful**
265. out the **closer   room's**
266. **formerly   Butterflies**
267. **braked**
268. **omit like**
269. **Junior High School**
270. way people **are screened for radiation exposure.**
271. **Upon entering federal buildings, place your metals in a screening basket.**
272. **kinds**
273. **After rereading the paragraph I still found it illogical.**
274. **What is the age for one not to be considered a minor in Texas?**
275. **led**
276. **densely-peopled   Nigerian**   its **many** inhabitants
277. **misspelled   pamphlet.**
278. **adolescent   ecstasy**

279. Americans," speech, "let time."
280. French
281. as **he**
282. **Imelda and I**
283. **But, we, him, realize history, dissimilar renaissance**
284. *A Man Named White*
285. **women themselves** and **macaroni and cheese.**
286. **"bling."**
287. **were** mine
288. **a part earth-friendly**
289. **continuously**
290. **given** a **screening** test
291. **As I drove around the mountains, I saw steep cliffs come into view.**
292. **is** in
293. **is** wilting
294. **are** going
295. **principal are** responsible
296. **is** difficult
297. **founded**
298. **omit of** and **it** White House
299. *The Real Housewives of DC* **has** been
300. **inalienable lose**

THEIR MUST BEE SUM WEIGH TOO NO
WITCH IS THE RITE WHEY

BONUS:

I never saw. his one-eyed tigers are his logo. trademark is a legal identification. a manufacturer uses any tactic to sell his clothing. a necessity of life is air.

AnnotationPress

A Division of WinePress Publishing

To order additional copies of this book call:
1-877-421-READ (7323)
or please visit our website at
www.annotationbooks.com

If you enjoyed this quality custom-published book,
drop by our website for more books and information.

www.winepresspublishing.com
"Your partner in custom publishing."

CPSIA information can be obtained at www.ICGtesting.com
Printed in the USA
BVOW041548090512

289730BV00001B/12/P